Islam: Faith and Practice

M. M. Ahsan

THE ISLAMIC FOUNDATION

© The Islamic Foundation, 1977
1397 A.H.
Reprinted 1980, 1981,1985 and 1991
ISBN 0 86037 001 1

Published by:
THE ISLAMIC FOUNDATION,
223 London Road,
Leicester, LE2 1ZE,
United Kingdom.
Tel: (0533) 700725

Quran House,
P.O. Box 30611,
Nairobi,
Kenya.

P.M.B. 3193,
Kano,
Nigeria.

Cover design by:
Sultan-ul-Hasan Farooqui

Sole Distributor In The Middle East And Asia:

INTERNATIONAL ISLAMIC PUBLISHING HOUSE

P.O Box 55195 Riyadh 11534 - Saudi Arabia - Tel. 4650818 - 4647213 - Fax 4633489

الموزع الوحيد في الشرق الأوسط وآسيا:

الدار العلمية للكتاب الإسلامي

ص.ب: ٥٥١٩٥ ـ الرياض ١١٥٣٤ ـ هاتف ٤٦٥٠٨١٨ ـ ٤٦٤٧٢١٣ ـ فاكس ٤٦٣٣٤٨٩

Contents

FOREWORD

It gives me great pleasure to write these few lines to introduce Dr. M. M. Ahsan's new book, *Islam: Faith and Practice*. Dr. Ahsan is a young, competent scholar and represents that new group of Islamic scholars who, on the one hand are deeply immersed in the age-old tradition of Islamic scholarship as developed in the Muslim world and on the other have penetrating familiarity with the mode of Western scholarship on Islam: its content as well as its methodology. It is hoped that through the efforts of scholars like him will be established a new tradition in the field of Islamic studies in the West wherein Islam will be understood and interpreted in the light of the pristine Islamic tradition and presented in a language that can be easily understood by the modern man.

Islam: Faith and Practice gives a bird's-eye view of Islam as a faith and a culture. The author has given a clear, concise and authentic exposition of the essentials of the Islamic faith and the various expressions of this faith in the life of the Muslims, as individuals and as a community. It covers a vast canvas with rare brevity and precision. It will be of immense help to those non-Muslims who want to have a general idea about Islam and the Muslim way of life. I am sure it will be read with interest and profit by those who want to know more about Islam.

The Islamic Foundation
1st October, 1976
6 Shawwāl, 1396

Khurshid Ahmad
Director General

4

Preface

Islam is perhaps the most abused as well as the most misunderstood religion in the West. Though oriental studies, especially the study of Islam, have received over the years a great deal of attention in European and American universities, real Islam, as Muslims believe and practise it, has seldom been presented to the world. No doubt voluminous works have been produced, a number of rare manuscripts edited and brought to light, encyclopaedias compiled, various conferences and seminars organized, numerous journals printed, yet one feels that real Islamic teachings have not been explained and if they have been, they have been presented in a wrong perspective leading to confusion and scepticism. Islam was equated with Muslim monarchs and people with little integrity and character and their ways of life were depicted as Islamic. Attempts are now being made to rectify this situation but they are so limited that it will take a long time to present Islam in its true perspective and remove the misconceptions surrounding it.

The present booklet aims at presenting Islam from its original sources and as the overwhelming majority of Muslims believe and practise it all over the world. This was originally compiled at the request of The Evangelical Alliance, London, to explain the basic beliefs and practices of Islam to non-Muslims. It has since been thoroughly revised and enlarged so that it can be used by students and others alike. A Muslim world map has been especially prepared for the book and inserted at the end to make the book more interesting and useful. The unique characteristic of the map lies in the fact that it is not only geographic but demographic, showing the Muslim population of the world in different colours. A chart of Muslim countries and those with signi-

5

ficant Muslim population has been appended for general interest and reference. I am greatly indebted to Professor Khurshid Ahmad, Mrs. D. Buckmaster and Mr. Yusuf Umar for thoroughly reading the manuscript and suggesting improvements. My thanks are also due to Mrs. Von Sicard and Mr. E. Fox for their valuable comments and suggestions and also to Brothers Sultan-ul-Hasan Farooqui and Wajihuddin Ahmad for taking unusual interest and devoting a great deal of their time in preparing the Muslim world map. Mrs. K. Hollingworth deserves special thanks for ungrudgingly typing the manuscript more than once.

The Islamic Foundation   M. M. Ahsan
27th August, 1976
1st Ramaḍān, 1396

1

Islam: Its Meaning

Islam is an Arabic word which means obedience, submission and peace. Islam is to commit one's self totally to God, making one's will subservient to and in complete harmony with the Will of God. Submission in Islam is not taken in any passive sense but as a positive act of committing one's self to live in peace with God and bringing one's likes and dislikes, one's attitudes and behaviour into harmony with the Divine Will. In simple words, a Muslim is one who adopts Islam as a way of life, follows God's commands and does not disobey Him in word or action.. In Arabic, God is called *Allāh*, which is also His proper name. Muslims all over the world prefer to use Allah in spite of having an equivalent word in their own language.[1]

The relationship between man and God is that of Master and servant, Creator and created, Ruler and ruled. Muslims look toward God as the only source of knowledge and guidance. God has made His Will known to people through His Messengers who received guidance from Him and communicated it to their people so that everybody could live a life of peace and happiness and seek the pleasure and approval of God.

---

1. Arabic speaking Christians, as also the Arabic edition of the Bible, use Allah for God.

2

Articles of Faith

Islamic life is based on two solid foundations: (a) belief and (b) action. Belief without action is of no use, nor is action without belief of any value. Both must go together and remain together.

There are three fundamental beliefs which form the basis of Islamic faith: the Oneness of God *(Tawḥīd)*, Prophethood *(Risāla)* and Life after Death *(Ākhira)*.

ONENESS OF GOD *(TAWḤĪD)*

Oneness of God, in Arabic *Tawḥīd*, means uncompromising and pure monotheism. Islam teaches that God is One and Unique. He is All-Powerful, Ruler and Master of all, who requires no partners nor has any offspring or family.[1] He is the *Rabb*, the Sustainer and the Nourisher of the entire world in whose hands are the life and death of all creatures. He is the Law-Giver and Administrator and He alone is worthy of praise and worship. Guidance necessarily should emanate from Him.

Human knowledge by its nature is incapable of deriving the guidance and the principles that can create equilibrium and balance within human society, thus harmonizing human behaviour with the cosmic dynamic equilibrium of forces. Investigation, observation and deduction cannot lead to an objective analysis within human society for the observer and the deducer is himself a human being and his perception of social phenomenon and social relation is necessarily subjective; reflecting his own biases, prejudices and belief. The

---

1. The Qur²ān 112: 1-4.

8

cognitive capacity of human beings is so limited, feeble and partial that it cannot serve as a reliable guide to the ultimate truth. Hence the guidance received from God can be the only criterion for right and wrong. Such guidance is incomparably superior to all man-made ideology as all of these are invariably marred by human prejudices in one form or other. God is external to and omnipotent over human society and the universe, hence He alone can be aware of the laws that can create social harmony within human society and the laws that can relate it harmoniously to its external universal environment.

PROPHETHOOD *(RISĀLA)* .

The second belief is in Prophethood. Following His providential system, God has provided mankind with all necessary guidance for its perennial physical and universal needs. This guidance has been handed over to Prophets who communicated it to their fellow beings not only in words but in action. A Muslim believes in the role the Prophets of God have played throughout history in communicating the message of God and demonstrating the way of life a man is supposed to follow.[1] The first man, Adam, was the first Prophet on this earth. The reason it was necessary to send Prophets at different times was to bring human beings back to the right path of God when they had strayed away. All the Prophets—Abraham, Isaac, Jacob, Moses, Solomon, David, John and Jesus, to mention only a few (peace be on all of them)—were chosen by God and were given one and the same message—'that God is One and His commands alone are to be obeyed by mankind'. God calls all these Prophets Muslims, because all of them followed the Right Path and were true and faithful servants of God.[2] The office of Prophethood came to an end with the last Prophet, Muhammad (peace be upon him). God made him to be the seal of all the Prophets by whom the religion of Islam, as a way of life, was completed.[3]

1. The Qur'ān 16: 36.
2. Ibid 3: 67; 2: 285; 3: 83-85; 22: 78; 5: 111.
3. Ibid 33: 40; 5: 3.

Some of the Prophets were granted scripture from God which contained detailed information about the way mankind should live to please God and to achieve salvation. The Torah was revealed to the Prophet Moses and the Gospel was given to the Prophet Jesus, and parts of these are available in the Old and New Testaments. The book of God which has been revealed to the Prophet Muhammad is known as the Qurʾān, which means the noble "Reading".

A Page from the Qurʾān.

Sūra al-Fātiha, *the first chapter of the Qurʾān, which every Muslim recites during the prayer.*

Translation:

In the name of God, the Merciful, the Mercy-Giving!
Praise be to God, Lord of the Universe,
the Merciful, the Mercy-Giving!
Ruler of the Day for Repayment!
You do we worship and from You do we seek help.
Guide us along the Straight Road,
the Road of those whom You have favoured,
with whom You are not angry,
And who are not lost!

The Opening *1: 1-7 (complete)*

10

The Qur'ān, being the last scripture of God, enshrines all the basic teachings of the earlier scriptures, whose original texts were lost and are now found only in recensions and translations.[1] The Qur'ān is the word of God revealed to the Prophet Muḥammad through the angel Jibra'īl (Gabriel), and is preserved and protected in the form in which it was revealed.[2] Thus it is the first and fundamental source of guidance and is followed by Muslims all over the world. It teaches that Jesus was not a son of God but His chosen Prophet, born of the Virgin Mary.[3] The Qur'ān is the foundation of Muslim life, which binds Muslims together, gives them a distinct identity and fashions their history and culture. It deals with all the important aspects of human life: the relationship between God and man, between man and man and between man and society, including ethics, jurisprudence, social justice, political principles, law, morality, trade and commerce.

The second source of guidance after the Qur'ān is the *Ḥadīth* (the Traditions), that is the sayings and actions of or approved by the Prophet Muḥammad, which have been preserved with remarkable accuracy and in minute detail. The Traditions of the Prophet Muḥammad present detailed commentary on the Qur'ān and represent a model of the Islamic way of life.[4] Muslims pattern their lives according to the rules laid down in the Qur'ān and the Traditions of the Prophet.

LIFE AFTER DEATH (ĀKHIRA)

The third fundamental belief in Islam after the Oneness of God and Prophethood is the belief in Life after Death. This present life on earth becomes meaningless if it is not followed by another life where reward and punishment are meted out to individuals on the basis of their previous lives. Muslims therefore believe in the Hereafter and the Day of

---

1. The Qur'ān 5: 48; 10: 37.
2. Ibid 15: 9; 53: 3-6.
3. Ibid 21: 91; 19: 16-36.
4. Ibid 33: 21; 59: 7.

11

Judgment where each individual will be called to account for his or her conduct and rewarded accordingly. Those who were good in this life will be given Paradise as a reward, whereas those who did not follow God's commands and lived unjustly will be punished in Hell.[1] Unlike the life on this earth, the life in the Hereafter will be infinite, that is it will never end.[2]

Belief in Life after Death is most crucial because it plays a tremendous role in the life of a Muslim. Since he believes that he will die and will be accountable to God in the Hereafter, he behaves altogether in a different way. Whenever he performs an action he first of all thinks whether his action is in accordance with God's command or not. This belief, therefore, creates God-consciousness in him and makes him live a decent and peaceful life on earth. A Muslim knows that if he misbehaves and appropriates the rights of others he cannot escape God's punishment on the Day of Judgment. God is Just and He will judge matters with justice and equity.

---

1. Ibid 2: 25, 39; 98: 6-8.
2. Ibid 4: 123; 78: 17.

3
Pillars of Islam

A man who has consciously accepted these beliefs is expected to follow them by actions which will complete his *Islām*. Belief in One God and His Messenger, Muḥammad constitutes the first pillar of Islam and is followed by four others involving practical obligations. These are Prayer, Fasting, Paying the Welfare Due and Pilgrimage. A brief outline of these pillars of Islam will perhaps be useful here to an understanding of the nature and scope of the Islamic faith and culture.

PRAYER *(ṢALĀT)*

Though a Muslim's whole life is a life of prayers and worship,[1] he is specifically required to pray five times a day; at dawn, after mid-day, in the late afternoon, after sunset and in the late evening when the last glow has left the sky.[2] Men are asked to pray at mosques in congregation.[3] In the absence of a mosque in the vicinity, they may pray at home, at their place of work or at any place which is neat and clean.[4] Women are encouraged to pray at home and not to take unnecessary trouble to attend the mosques.[5]

There is no priesthood in Islam. Any Muslim who is well-versed in Islamic teachings can lead the prayers. Knowledge of the Qurʾān and purity of character are essential qualifications for one who leads the prayers.[6] The five daily prayers make a Muslim remember God constantly, keep him away from evil and misconduct and induce in him high moral and physical discipline.[7] Prayer in congre-

---

1. The Qurʾān 51: 56.
2. Ibid 11: 114; 17: 78-80; 20: 130-32; see also Bukhārī, *Ḥadīth* No. 7.
3. Cf. Muslim, chapter "Prayer in Congregation".
4. Bukhārī, *Ḥadīth* No. 429.
5. Cf. *Mishkāt* and books on *Fiqh*.
6. Cf. Muslim.
7. The Qurʾān 29: 45.

gation inculcates the values of brotherhood, social responsibility, community spirit and discipline in thought and action. Muslims in their prayer face towards the Ka'ba in Makka.

The direction of the Ka'ba *(Qibla* in Arabic) naturally varies from country to country. For example, those living in China, India, Pakistan and other countries in the east will face towards the west, while those in Russia will face towards the south, and those in Africa will face towards the north. Muslims in Britain and adjoining countries face towards the south-east. On Fridays, in lieu of the mid-day prayer, Muslims all over the world offer special Friday Prayers in congregation. This is obligatory for all Muslims.[1]

Prayer is such an obligatory duty that it cannot be waived even in time of war, or when one is ill or on a journey.[2] Special regulations have been given for the performance of the prayer under these circumstances.[3] However, women during menstruation as well as in the post-natal period are exempt from prayers.

Cleanliness of the body, clothes and place of worship is an essential requirement for the offering of the prayer.[4] Muslims, therefore, take great care to ensure that their bodies and their clothes are clean and are not soiled from any external or internal source. In religious terms, one's body or clothes become polluted when coming into contact with unclean substances such as excrement, urine, blood, pus, wine, etc.[5] Uncleanliness does not include the normal dust acquired in the day's work but only the substances just mentioned.

---

1. The Qur'ān 62: 9.
2. It is obligatory that Muslims working in factories, offices, etc. should offer their prayer at appointed times. Therefore facilities should be provided and they should be allowed time to pray.
3. The Qur'ān 4: 101-102.
4. Ibid 74: 4-5.
5. See books of *Ḥadīth* and *Fiqh,* chapter "*Ṭahāra*".

14

A group of Muslims offering their prayer in congregation (Jamāᶜa).

Position of qiyām (standing)

Position of rukūᶜ (bowing on the knee)

Position of sajda (prostration)   *(Photographs by Rashid Khan)*

A ceremonial ablution, that is the washing of hands up to the elbow, rinsing the mouth, washing the face and feet up to the ankles and passing the wet hand over the head—all done in a specific order—is pre-requisite for the validity of the prayer.[1] This wash is known as *Wuḍū°* and is performed before each prayer. The *Wuḍū°* becomes void and must be done again if one answers the call of nature, releases wind, sleeps, vomits or bleeds from any cut or injury.[2] After any ejaculation, termination of menstruation and post-natal periods, a full bath is taken and the body is ceremonially cleaned.[3] If there is any external form of pollution on the body or on the clothes, that part is washed until the stains are obliterated.

FASTING *(ṢAWM)*

The fast in Islam is not performed for any worldly gain or to obtain any political concessions. It is observed purely as an act of worship *(ᶜibāda)*, to obey the commands of God and to show that Muslims are ready to respond to the call of their Lord at any time and under any circumstances. Every male and female who has attained puberty has to fast by way of abstaining from food, drink, smoking and sexual intercourse from dawn to sunset during the lunar month of Ramaḍān.[4] The lunar month of Ramaḍān moves forward ten or eleven days each year against the solar year, so that the month of fasting falls over the years both in summer and winter. This is also one of the reasons that Islam has never become involved with seasonal pagan practices, such as fertility cults.

---

1. See chapter *"Ṭahāra"* in *Ḥadīth* and *Fiqh* literature.
2. A detailed discussion on cleanliness and the causes which necessitate a bath or ablution and the forms of obtaining ritual purification will be discussed in a forthcoming publication.
3. The Qurʾān 5: 6. See also chapter *"Ṭahāra"* in *Ḥadīth* and *Fiqh* literature.
4. The Qurʾān 2: 183-187.

The fast is a unique form of worship where there cannot be any element of display, which is possible in other forms of worship. This is why God declared: "Fasting is for Me, and I am sufficient for its reward".[1] That fasting alone is of merit, which is kept with the utmost sense of duty, refraining from all sorts of evil in thought and action. Otherwise, the man who fasts will have no more than hunger and thirst.[2] Fasting in Islam produces a sound conscience and strong moral and civic responsibility. It teaches one to be kind to the poor and needy, and to experience and share willingly the hardship and sufferings of the poor. It enables one to control and restrain passion and helps one to acquire piety and heedfulness of God. It brings one closer to God and gives great spiritual strength. Fasting is therefore a higher form of spiritual training which makes the path of obedience easier. It also offers an opportunity to commemorate the beginning of the revelation of the Qurʾān which happened in the month of Fasting, Ramaḍān,[3] about thirteen years before the Prophet's migration from Makka to Madina.

The fast lasts for twenty nine or thirty days, depending on when the new moon is sighted. Fasting is an obligatory form of worship which can be deferred only by a person who is ill, a traveller, women in menstruation or the post-natal period, or nursing a baby, etc. They have to make up the number of fast days thus missed, outside the month of Ramaḍān.[4] Usually, Muslims rise a couple of hours before sunrise and have an early meal called Suḥūr so as to provide them with some nourishment for the rest of the day.[5]

1. Cf. Bukhārī and Muslim. chapter "Fasting"
2. Ibid.
3. The Qurʾān 2: 185.
4. See the books on Fiqh, chapter "Fasting".
5. Cf. Bukhārī and Muslim, chapter "Fasting"

THE WELFARE DUE (ZAKĀT)

Zakāt or the "welfare money", has been mentioned in the Qurʾān as a "claim" of the poor on the wealth of the rich.[1] This payment purifies the wealth as well as the attitude and feelings of the person paying.[2] *Zakāt* is an act of worship, hence one should not show any sign of pride or of doing a favour in giving away one's money to those who are in need. In fact, the underlying idea is that through this process wealth reaches those to whom it belongs.

In Islam, wealth is held in trust from God, hence every prosperous Muslim is obliged to share his wealth with those in need, so that a balanced economic life may be developed in the community. *Zakāt* is one of the means of achieving this end. It is an obligatory annual financial contribution to individuals or to the Islamic State of at least two and a half per cent of one's annual savings, merchandise and jewels, etc.[3] This amount is used to raise the living standard of the poorer members of the community. Being an act of conscience, this contribution from the rich to the poor is not evaded by anybody and therefore needs no official inspection. It is given out in the spirit of a *duty* and not as charity. Charity is paid additionally.

Zakāt is paid by individuals to Islamic Governments, who arrange for its proper distribution to deserving people. In the absence of an Islamic Government, it is paid either to Islamic organizations, who take the responsibility of collecting and distributing it to deserving persons or to family members resident in the country or abroad. According to the teachings of the Qurʾān, poverty and affluence are both trials from God. Success lies in moderation and restraint.[4]

---

1. The Qurʾān 51: 19; 9: 60.
2. Ibid 9: 103.
3. See the books of *Ḥadīth* and *Fiqh*, chapter *"Zakāt"*.
4. The Qurʾān 5: 48; 6: 165; 21: 35; 12: 29; 25: 67.

PILGRIMAGE *(ḤAJJ)*

Pilgrimage is enjoined only on those adults who are able to afford it and who are physically fit to travel to Makka, a city blessed for having the Kaʿba, the House of God, originally built by the Prophet Abraham about three thousand years ago.[1] Pilgrimage is obligatory only once in a lifetime, though the believers cherish and perform it as many times as

The Kaʿba (House of God). Every year more than a million Muslims perform their Pilgrimage here. Muslims all over the world face this house in their prayer.

(Photo: Anis Ahmad)

---

1. The Qurʾān 2: 127, 197.

possible. Muslims from all over the world, from different nationalities, ethnic origins, colour and language gather together in a spirit of worship and dedication to God and perform special religious rites from the eighth to the thirteenth, Dhū'l-Ḥijja, the last month of the Islamic calendar. The assembly of Muslims at the time of Pilgrimage demonstrates Muslim unity, brotherhood and equality at its best. Pilgrims of every hue, whether rich or poor, literate or illiterate, powerful or weak, ruler or ruled, wear the same type of unsewn cloth and perform the same religious rites, standing and bowing, shoulder to shoulder.

One of the features of the *Hajj* is the sacrifice of animals made in commemoration of the Prophet Abraham, who readily responded to his Lord's call to sacrifice his son Ishmael some three thousand years ago.[1] By performing this sacrifice Muslims exhibit their willingness to sacrifice their lives and property for the sake of God. This unique view of the equality of mankind and congregational worship on such a large scale as one finds in the Pilgrimage is something special to Islam, which no religion on earth can rival. The Pilgrimage also represents an international annual gathering of Muslims, where about two million pilgrims meet each other and have an opportunity to exchange their views and learn from the experiences of one another.

---

1. The Qur'ān 37: 102; see also the books of *Hadīth* and *Fiqh*, chapter "*Hajj* and *Udhiyya*".

4

Islamic Way of Life

The life of a Muslim is a life led in complete and total obedience to the commandments of God. Islam is a religion of broader spectrum than is the case with other religions. It provides a complete and comprehensive code for the conduct of human life from the cradle to the grave. It is a force in itself, having the potentiality for guidance in all spheres of life for the individual and to the entire population of the world as a whole. It provides guidance in all social, economic, political, moral and spiritual aspects of life. The purpose of human life on earth, man's duties and obligations towards himself, his kith and kin and to society, and towards the Creator, have all been clearly expounded.[1]

Islam does not divide life into what is sacred and what is secular. Every aspect of life has been taken into consideration and guidance has been provided in all fields. Hence every action of a Muslim can be regarded as worship (*ᶜibāda*) if it is done with the intention of fulfilling God's commands. Earning one's livelihood by engaging in a trade, or in a skilled or unskilled profession may be a secular act in other faiths, but it is an act of worship in Islam, provided it is undertaken in the right spirit and with commitment to the values established by Islam.[2] Islam has clearly demarcated the limits of lawful and unlawful things and has asked Muslims not to approach the prohibited things.[3] The injunctions of the Qurᵓān were translated into practice by the Prophet Muhammad (peace be upon him) thus providing a living model for all.[4] Man has thus been given the funda-

---

1. See the Qurᵓān 5: 3; 3: 19; 6: 38. See also the books of *Ḥadīth*.
2. See for example, Bukhārī and other *Ḥadīth* literature.
3. The Qurᵓān 6: 151; 17: 32, 34; 2: 187.
4. Ibid 33: 21; 7: 157-158. See also *Musnad* of Ibn Ḥanbal, VI, No. 188 and Muslim.

mental rules for leading a peaceful life. He has been equipped with high moral values and standards. Attainment of high moral and spiritual discipline through the prescribed forms of worship enables him to accept all challenges, to face any crisis and to endure all trials and tribulations.

Islam does not uphold the idea that man is born in sin, and that as such he needs somebody to atone for his offences. On the contrary, it teaches that every man is born naturally a Muslim on the *fitra*,[1] hence free from sin, and equal in status with all other men. Similarly the division of mankind into different races, nations and tribes is not meant to create strife and division but to help men recognize and co-operate with one another. The man of honour and esteem in the eyes of God is he who is most dutiful to God. A Qurʾānic verse very beautifully puts the point in the following words:

> "O mankind, We have created you from a single pair of male and female, and set you up as nations and tribes, so that you may know one another. The noblest of you before God are the most heedful of you".[2]

Muslims are therefore a single brotherhood who co-operate with each other on the basis of piety and righteousness and do not participate in vice and aggression.[3] There is no distinction or discrimination on the basis of colour, race, nationality or ethnic background. In fact, Islam unites all men and makes them abandon their old prejudices and superstitions, making them a single community, a Muslim *Umma*. In a Prophetic *Ḥadīth* (Traditional saying) Muslims have been compared to the body—if one part of it aches, the whole body feels its effect and rushes to its relief.[4]

---

1. Every child is born naturally a Muslim, but is perverted after birth by his environment. Cf. *Mishkāt*, Vol. 1.
2. The Qurʾān 49: 13.
3. Ibid 5: 2.
4. Bukhārī and Muslim.

A Muslim's love of God and his fellow beings is not passive in the sense that one may pay only lip service to God and behave indifferently to His commands. In fact a Muslim is expected to love God and His Prophet more than he loves his own self, his parents, children and wives, and to demonstrate that love in the form of action, making his will completely subservient to the Will of God and to the Prophet.[1] Indeed his actions are a yardstick to measure his love for God.

Having described in some detail the basic articles of faith and the pillars of Islam and seen how the Islamic law governs the entire gamut of Muslim life, we may now turn to what can be termed the practical aspects of life and see what Islam has to offer in matters of festivals, social manners, diet, dress, etc.

---

1. Cf. Bukhārī and Muslim.

5

Festivals and Festivities in Islam

Islam has two major festivals a year, one at the end of the month of Fasting known as ʿĪd al-Fiṭr, and the other towards the end of the Pilgrimage period when all those who do not attend the Pilgrimage celebrate a Festival of Sacrifice known as ʿĪd al-Aḍḥā.

ʿĪD AL-FIṬR

The Festival of the ʿĪd al-Fiṭr marks the end of the fast and on that day the community offers special congregational prayer and it is customary to visit one's friends and relatives, all of whom participate in the joyous occasion. Children receive gifts, new clothes and presents, while others exchange greetings and wear their best clothes on this Festive day. It is an obligation on every Muslim who is not poor to give charity to the poorer members of society to enable them to enjoy the celebration in a decent manner.[1] The Festival of the ʿĪd al-Fiṭr is a time of thanksgiving to God for enabling Muslims to observe the fast of the whole month of Ramaḍān and seeking His forgiveness for any lapses. Muslim festivals differ sharply from the festivals of other religions in the sense that Islam does not allow its followers to indulge in extravagance, attend concerts, dances, wine parties, or discotheques and such worldly pleasures. It is an occasion for prayer, social greetings and reunions.

---

1. Cf. Abū Dāwūd. See also other Hadīth and Fiqh literature, chapter "ʿĪd".

24

The scene of Sacrifice of Animals at Mina during the Pilgrimage period. Muslims slaughter the animal by the inner part of the neck, using a sharp knife. (From the Ḥajj folder published by Minaret House, Croydon.)

ʿĪD AL-AḌḤĀ (Festival of Sacrifice)

The ʿĪd al-Aḍḥā occurs towards the end of the Pilgrimage period and is also an occasion when Muslims throughout the world attend congregational prayers and make a sacrifice to God in the form of an animal, sharing its meat with relatives, friends, and the poor. By observing this Festival, Muslims demonstrate their readiness to sacrifice their lives as did the Prophet Abraham about three thousand years ago. This Festival is celebrated for three days. As with the Festival of ʿĪd al-Fiṭr, schools, colleges, universities and government offices, as well as private institutions in the Muslim countries, remain closed during these days so that everybody can participate in the celebration and enjoy lawful things in a relaxed mood.[1]

---

1. A great number of Muslims are now living in non-Muslim countries, such as Europe, America and Australia, hence the majority community in such countries should recognize the cultural and religious needs of the Muslims living there. Muslims of such countries have the right to at least a day off to celebrate the major festivals. Denying them this right is tantamount to an infringement of basic human rights.

Apart from these two festivals, there are some other occasions which Muslims all over the world celebrate with much enthusiasm. Strictly speaking they are not festivals and some of them were not even celebrated by the Prophet and the early Muslim community. However such festive occasions are as follows:

(a) LAYLAT AL-QADR (The Night of Power)

Laylat al-Qadr, described in the Qur²ān as "better than a thousand months",[1] occurs on one of the five odd nights in the last ten days of Ramaḍān.[2] The night of the 27th is regarded as the likeliest night of *Qadr,* and elaborate preparations are made to welcome this night with prayer and devotion. This blessed night is traditionally observed in all parts of the Muslim world with great reverence. Muslims devote the whole night to offering supererogatory prayers, reading from the Qur²ān, visiting the cemetery and asking forgiveness from God.

(b) ῾ĀSHŪRĀ² (Tenth of Muḥarram)

῾Āshūrā² is observed on the tenth of Muḥarram, the first month of the Muslim calendar. On this day, Muslims observe a voluntary fast and in some parts of the Muslim world they celebrate it by preparing special dishes. To differentiate from the one-day fast of the Jews, Muslims celebrate *Āshūrā²* by fasting for two days. Historically the day of *Āshūrā²* is of immense importance, because it was on this day that the Prophet Noah left the ark, the Prophet Moses saved the Israelites from the Pharaohs.[3]

---

1. The Qur²ān 97: 3.
2. See Bukhārī and Muslim, s.v. *Ramaḍān* and *Qadr.*
3. Bukhārī and Muslim, s.v. *῾Āshūrā²*

London Central Mosque, situated at 146 Park Road, London, N.W.8. One of the biggest Mosques and Islamic Centres in Europe. (By courtesy of Publication Department, Islamic Cultural Centre, London.)

(c) JUM ᶜAT AL-WADĀᶜ (Farewell Friday)

Historically Jumᶜa (Friday) has always been a day of special religious significance especially marked by Friday congregational prayer.[1] *Jumᶜat al-Wadāᶜ* occurring on the last Friday of Ramaḍān is of special significance. On this day, Muslims in large numbers throng to mosques and offer their prayers in congregation, bidding farewell to the month of Fasting with a heavy heart.

(d) LAYLAT AL-MIᶜRĀJ (Night of the Ascent)

The celebration of *Laylat al-Miᶜrāj* is made to commemorate the ascent of the Prophet Muḥammad to Heaven.[2] The *Miᶜrāj* also known as the *Isrāʾ*, happened on the 27th of Rajab, the seventh month of the Muslim calendar in the tenth year of Muḥammad's prophethood. On this particular date, Muslims hold special assemblies and describe the life of the Prophet with special reference to the *Miᶜrāj*.

1. The Qur'ān 62: 9.
2. The Prophet led by the Archangel Jibra'īl was taken to the Seven Heavens where he spoke with God and came back the same night with a number of instructions such as the institution of the obligatory five daily prayers. See *Hadīth literature on Mi'rāj. The celebration of this night is a later development in Islam.*

27

(e) MAWLID AN-NABĪ (Birthday of the Prophet)

The ʿĪd Mawlid an-Nabī is celebrated with special assemblies organized to eulogize the Prophet and describe different aspects of his life.[1] Sometimes, Muslims organize such functions to last over several days in the month of Rabīᶜ al-Awwal, the third month of the Muslim calendar, in which the Prophet was born.

There are some other festive occasions connected with the family such as the birth of a child, circumcision and marriage. It is part of the Islamic faith that a child is received as a gift from God and is not to be considered, as some Westerners think of them as a "Problem".[2] For this reason, the birth of a child is considered a great blessing and consequently, Muslims express their thanks by giving to the poor gifts in the form of food, money or clothes, announcing the name of God (Adhān) in the infant's ears and arranging an ᶜAqīqa party, usually after a week, where an animal is sacrificed and friends and relatives are invited to a feast.[3]

The circumcision of a boy (khitān) is another occasion for festivity in the family. It is said that the practice of circumcision, which has been made obligatory in Islam, has been inherited from the Prophet Abraham.[4] The boy is attired in good clothes and receives presents from relatives and well-wishers. Often, to mark the occasion, the parents also arrange a feast to which friends, relatives and neighbours are invited.

---

1. The celebration of the Prophet's birthday in Muslim society started from the 10th Century C.E. i.e., about four hundred years after the death of the Prophet. (cf. Mez, *Renaissance of Islam*, Eng. tr. by Khuda Bakhsh, London, 1937, p.427).
2. See *Mishkāt*, chapter " *Aqīqa*", where a number of Traditional sayings have been quoted.
3 Ibid.
4 See for example, *Mishkāt* and books on *Fiqh*.

28

6

Marriage and Family

Marriage is the basis of social life and the beginning of family life. Islam considers marriage to be a very sacred act and a step towards a better, purer and happier life.[1] Marriages are usually arranged by the parents and the wedding is attended by the parents of the bride and groom and guests, consisting of relatives of both families, as well as friends and neighbours. The wedding ceremony itself is simple but magnificent. The bride and bridegroom, attired in splendid clothes, appear with their entourage at the wedding place, either the residence of the bride or a mosque, and give their consent to the marriage before two witnesses. The person who conducts the marriage, often known as *Qāḍī*,[2] announces the amount of the dowry which the bridegroom has to offer to the bride and invokes a blessing on them by reciting from the Qurʾān and Traditions of the Prophet, known as *Khuṭba*.[3] Sweets, usually in the form of dates, are distributed among those present at the wedding which is generally followed by a banquet. The bridegroom takes the bride home and the next day he arranges a *walīma* party inviting friends, relatives and well-wishers to a sumptuous meal.

Islam condemns pre-marital sex, and the free mixing of grown-up boys and girls is not allowed. Hence, in an Islamic society, there is no such concept as "unmarried mother" or "bachelor father". The penalty for pre-marital and post-marital immorality is severe indeed.[4] In certain cases Islam

---

1. The Qurʾān 4: 25; 24: 32-33; 30: 21; 7: 189.
2. Literally, Judge. In the Indo-Pak sub-continent the title *Qāḍī* is used for the registrar of the marriage.
3. Ibid 2: 236; 4: 4, 24. See also *Ḥadīth* literature, chapter "Marriage".
4. The Qurʾān 24: 2-3.

permits polygamy, as this helps to protect society from promiscuity and prostitution.[1] No discrimination is made on the basis of sex. Wife and husband are equal partners and both play an equal, though not similar, role in the shaping of the family and society.[2] If a marriage has broken down, divorce is permitted, although it is regarded as the most abominable of the permitted actions.[3] Cases of divorce are so rare in Muslim families that it does not pose any problem to society, as is the case in the West.

---

1. The Qur'ān 4: 3, 129
2. Ibid 2: 228; 4: 34. See also Khurshid Ahmad, *Family Life in Islam*, Islamic Foundation Publications, 1975.
3. Ibid 2: 229, 231; see also *Hadīth* and *Fiqh* literature, chapter "Divorce".

7

Ethics and Etiquette

Islam teaches man to be a decent and well-behaved member of society. Everybody should do his duty and respect others' feelings, emotions and rights, thus creating a society full of peace and tranquility. Whenever a Muslim meets another, be he his relative, a friend or a stranger, he greets him with a salutation, saying *As-salāmu ʿAlaykum,* (peace be on you). The other person replies, saying *Wa-ʿalaykum as-salām* (peace also be on you).[1]

Privacy and individual freedom have been given a unique place in Islam. Muslims are not allowed to enter another person's house without asking for permission. Indeed it discourages them from visiting each other at inconvenient times.[2] Keeping one's word, speaking the truth, dealing with justice and equity, helping orphans and the poor, are some of the virtues which Islam prizes most.[3]

Enmity and character assassination are considered as sinful as the physical destruction of life. Slander, blasphemy, ridicule, use of offensive names, suspicion and such things have been forbidden in Islam, as these things tear men from one another and create a wedge in society.[4] The Qurʾānic statement, "O you who believe! Avoid suspicion, for suspicion in some cases is a sin, and spy not on each other, nor speak ill of each other behind their backs. Would any of you like to eat the flesh of his dead brother?"[5] — indicates the

---

1. See the Qurʾān 4: 86.
2. Ibid 24: 27-28.
3. Ibid 2: 177; 4: 58; 6: 153; 9: 149; 16: 90-91.
4. Ibid 49: 11.
5. Ibid 49: 12.

abhorrence of destruction of character which applies to all men irrespective of their background, social position or family. Kind treatment of parents, particularly in their old age has been especially enjoined in Islam. Giving guidance on this point, the Qur'ān says:

"And show kindness to your parents; whether one or both of them attain old age (while they are) still with you, never say to them: 'Shame!' nor scold either of them. Speak to them in a generous fashion. Protect them carefully from outsiders and say: 'My Lord show them mercy, just as they cared for me as a little child' ".[1]

This instruction has such a bearing on Muslim life that the elders are regarded as the most respected members in the family and often make the final decision in all important matters.[2] In Islam, there is no problem of "old people's homes" because the old are not kept in isolation but cared for and looked after within the family.

---

1. Ibid 17: 23-24.
2. In fact, a Prophetic Tradition regards a man outside the pale of Islam if he does not show respect to the elders. The *Hadīth* says: "He who does not respect the elders and love the youngers is not of the Muslims". Cf. *Mishkāt.*

8

Dress

Islam has not prescribed any particular dress. It has given broad outlines and enjoined Muslims to cover their bodies properly and decently. Addressing mankind, God says:

"O Children of Adam, We have revealed to you (the knowledge of making) garments to cover your nakedness and as a thing of beauty; but the garment of God-consciousness is the best of all".[1]

The minimum part of the body that should necessarily be covered (*ᶜawra*) for a man is from his navel to his knees and for a woman from her head to her feet, leaving only the face and hands.[2] As to the shape of the garment, its colour and design, etc., no particular instructions have been given. They have been left to the requirement and choice of the individual. A Prophetic Tradition simply advises Muslims to avoid, among other things, imitating the costumes and fashions of other nations.[3] The emphasis is on simple dress and the suggestion is that the character of the man is more important than his dress.

It is because of this broad outline that we find different varieties of costumes used by Muslims in different parts of the world. Certainly climatic conditions and local customs play an important part in determining the clothing styles of

---

1. The Qurᵓān 7: 26.
2. See *Fiqh* literature on this point. Some scholars of Islam maintain that the face of the woman should be veiled while out of doors.
3. See for example, *Mishkāt*, chapter "Dress".

Muslims. In early Islam, the use of the turban as a headgear was very common, though it has lost its importance in recent times, but the flowing garments of earlier periods are still used in many parts of the Muslim world. Women going outdoors generally wear a special kind of veil which covers the head and some part of the face, which is.regarded as a mark of dignity and respect. Under no circumstances are they allowed to leave their legs uncovered.[1]

---

1. Muslims living in the U.K. and other non-Muslim countries face great problems when their daughters in schools and colleges are asked to use skirts or even mini-skirts as their uniform. This constitutes an encroachment on their religious and cultural rights. They should be given the choice to wear either a long skirt or trousers (shalwār).

9
Dietary Rules

As a rule, all good and wholesome things have been regarded as lawful *(halāl)* for Muslims to eat and drink. The things which have been prohibited *(harām)* for obvious reasons are few. They are (a) dead animals, (b) swine, (c) animals not ritually slaughtered, such as those killed by electric shock or sacrificed on a name other than that of God, (d) all carnivorous animals whether they are ritually slaughtered or not, and (e) blood.[1]

According to the Islamic law, the animal should be slaughtered by a sharp knife penetrating the inner part of the animal's neck while the name of God is invoked.[2] If God's name is not spoken with intent at the time of the slaughter the meat will not be regarded as *halāl* (pure and lawful).[3] The "Kosher" meat of the Jews may be eaten by Muslims if they slaughter their animals ritually and mention the name of God over them. Not only the meat but also anything procured from animals not ritually slaughtered or unclean animals, such as fat, marrow, etc. cannot be used in Muslim food.[4] Hence any preparation such as crisps with bacon flavour, cakes or biscuits, cheese or ice cream where animal fat has been used as an ingredient cannot be eaten by Muslims. Any dish fried with lard or other kinds of animal fat is likewise not lawful for Muslims to eat.[5] All varieties of fish are, however, perfectly lawful for the Muslim diet.

---

1. The Qur'ān 16:. 115. See also *Hadīth* and *Fiqh* literature where detailed regulations are described.
2. See *Fiqh* literature, chapter "Slaughtering of Animals".
3. The Qur'ān 6: 121.
4. The hide of such animals can be used after tanning. (cf *Fiqh* books).
5. Muslims living in the U.K. and other non-Muslim countries make special arrangements for slaughtering animals. They run their own *halāl* (Kosher) meat shops and prepare crisps, cakes, biscuits, bread, etc. either using butter, purified ghee or vegetable oil. They will not buy any food from the market unless they are sure of the purity of the ingredients.

All kinds of alcoholic drinks such as spirits and wine and other intoxicants, such as drugs, are completely prohibited in Islam.[1] All forms of non-alcoholic drink are however, lawful. Islam is so firm against alcohol that even if a drop of it is mixed in any food or drink, the whole of it becomes unclean. Wine, like gambling and raffles, has been declared foul and unwholesome by the Qur'ān. The pertinent verse of the Qur'ān reads:

> "You who believe, liquor and gambling, idols and raffles are only a filthy work of Satan; avoid them so that you may prosper. Satan only wants to stir up enmity and jealousy among you by means of liquor and gambling, and to hinder you from remembering God and from praying. So will you stop?"[2]

Islam strikes at the root of evil rather than its branches. That is why things which may create an adverse effect on health and society have been totally prohibited. Little use of these things may not show an immediate adverse effect, but continual use gradually makes a man an addict and leads him to moral failings and crimes. The moral and spiritual crises of the Western world lend support to this fact. Islam therefore cautions its followers not to even approach the bounds of prohibitions.

Islam prescribes decent rules for table manners. Muslims all over the world use their fingers to eat their food.[3] They wash their hands and rinse their mouths before and after each meal.[4] The after-meal wash sometimes becomes elaborate, involving the use of soap, necessary to remove the grease from the fingers. A toothpick is used to clean the teeth, which are washed thoroughly after every meal. Food is served from the right and eating is usually started by the eldest member of the family or the guest.[5]

---

1. The Qur'ān 5: 90-91. A Traditional saying of the Prophet provides a general guideline saying: "all that which intoxicates is unlawful" (cf. for example *Mishkāt*, chapter "Food and Drink".)
2. Ibid 5: 90-91.
3. The use of a spoon or fork, however, is permitted.
4. See for example, *Mishkāt*, chapter "Food".
5. Ibid.

The most important table manner is that one should start the meal with the name of God saying "In the name of God, the Merciful and the Beneficent" and recite a thanksgiving prayer after the meal, which is as follows:

"All praise be to Him who has given us to eat and drink and made us Muslims".[1]

Muslims eat with their right hand. It is regarded as discourteous to leave the table before the last person has finished his meal. Similarly, it is considered bad etiquette to talk too much or blow one's nose while taking food. It was a custom in the past which is still practised in some rural parts of the Arab world that a group of people eat from one large plate, sitting around it. Wastage of food is prohibited in Islam, hence it is recommended that everybody should cleanly finish the contents of their plate.

---

1. If one is invited to a meal, one should also add the following supplication: "O God, feed him who has fed me and give him more who has given me to drink and keep him firm in Islam". Cf. *Mishkāt*, chapter "Food".

10

Death and Burial

Death is always a time of grief for the members of the family, but not necessarily for the person dying. Though he suffers from the pangs of death, he feels a kind of happiness, when he realises that he is going to a world everlasting, full of bliss and enjoyment, the Heaven where he will be able to see God as well as all his relatives and friends.[1]

A Muslim on his death-bed tries to ask forgiveness (tawba) from God for all the offences he might have committed in his life and reads from the Qurʾān whatever passages he knows by heart.[2] His relatives and friends also ask forgiveness from God and invoke blessings by reciting the verses of the Qurʾān loudly. The last word of the Muslim is the Kalima,[3] the solemn affirmation of his faith in One God, saying:

> "There is no god but Allah, and Muhammad is His Messenger"

and also

> "I declare that there is no god but Allah and I bear witness that Muhammad is the Messenger of Allah".

---

1. The Qurʾān, see among many verses 3: 133-36; 47: 15; see also Bukhārī and Muslim as quoted in Mishkāt, chapter XIV, "The Vision of God Most High".
2. The Qurʾān 3: 133; see also Tirmidhī.
3. See for example, Mishkāt, chapter "Burial" (what to say for one who is dying).

38

After death has occurred the body is taken for bathing. The corpse is ritually washed with scented water and wrapped in simple white sheets.[1] The number of cloth pieces for a man is three and for a woman five. All the cloths are unsewn, there being no difference between rich and poor.[2] Once the deceased man is washed and wrapped, he is placed in a carrier like a cot and taken to a mosque or an open place where the members of the family and of the local community gather and offer a special funeral prayer. The prayer may be led by the *Imām* of the mosque or anybody from the family. After the prayer is over, the body is taken to the cemetery for burial.[3]

There is no hard and fast rule as to how soon a body should be buried. It depends on the time needed for the funeral arrangements, bathing and enwrapping in sheets. Islam forbids for the body to be kept at home for any longer than necessary and encourages its believers to bury it as early as possible.

Muslims do not bury their dead in a coffin: they dig a grave the size of a man and lay the body there facing towards the Ka‘ba. They then cover the grave with soil. When the body is lowered into the grave, these words are said:

"In the name of God, (we bury) according to the way of the Prophet of God".[4]

At the time of filling the grave with earth, these words are recited from the Qur’ān:

"We created you from it and deposit you into it and from it will take you out once more".[5]

---

1. See *Ḥadīth* and *Fiqh* literature, chapter "Washing and Wrapping a Dead Body".
2. Ibid.
3. Ibid, chapter "Funeral Prayer".
4. Ibid, chapter "Burial".
5. The Qur’ān 20: 55.

These words convey the spirit of Islamic culture and the attitude of mind Islam produces in its followers. There is no ceremony of wailing or mourning in the family, though everybody looks sad and grieved. As soon as the news of death spreads, the relatives, neighbours and well-wishers assemble in the house and console the members of the family, reminding them that all human beings belong to God and all have eventually to return to Him. They also pray for the departed soul and ask God to give strength and patience to the bereaved family to bear their loss.[1] Muslims are not allowed to erect any tombstone or building over the grave.[2]

See *Mishkāt,* chapter "Funeral" (Weeping for the Dead).
Cf. *Ḥadīth* literature.

11

Islam and the Present World

There are over forty two Muslim states in the present world, stretching over the three continents of Asia, Africa and Europe. The entire sub-continent of India, and a considerable part of Europe, including the Iberian Peninsula, were under Muslim rule for several hundred years. The Middle East and North Africa have traditionally been Muslim lands. The total world population of Muslims amounts to over eight hundred million.[1] In Europe, there are at present between twenty five and thirty million Muslims with a significant Muslim presence in almost every European country, including Communist ones. Muslims in the United Kingdom are estimated at approximately one million.[2]

Islam has proved over the past fourteen hundred years to be a living historic force. The achievements of Muslims in the fields of natural science, medicine, astronomy, mathematics, technology, *belles lettres,* art and architecture and above all in human thought and action — all designed to glorify the faith of Islam — can vividly be seen in their fourteen hundred years of history from Morocco to the Philippines, from Dar-es-Salam to Samarkand. In the past, the Islamic world surpassed Western Europe in both scholarship and technology and passed on their skill and knowledge (for example, the technique of paper-making,

---

1. For a demographic study of the Muslim world, see *World Muslim Gazetteer,* Umma Publication, Karachi, Pakistan, 1975 edition. The study puts the present world population of Muslims at 900 million. See also, *The Europa Year Book, 1976,* Europa Publications, London.
2. Cf. Khurshid Ahmad, *Muslims in Europe,* 1976.

the use of ciphers and numbers in arithmetic, the institution of universities and hospitals, etc.) to the world at large, leaving an everlasting mark on human civilization and culture.[1]

In the West, the message of Islam has been obscured either by wilful misunderstanding or through the legacy of the Crusades, yet it has survived all the vicissitudes of time. Islam, being the universal religion meant for mankind of all races, colours and times, is as relevant today as it was fourteen hundred years ago. It has been a great liberating force in the past and has the potential for leading man out of the contemporary crisis of human civilization. It was their faith which gave Muslims glory in the past and even today it is the only real source of their strength. In the context of contemporary spiritual and cultural crises, Islam provides an alternative basis for the development of human personality and the organization of human society. Peace and happiness remain elusive in spite of man's development with materialism, communism, secularism and other man-made cults. Peace and happiness in human life can be achieved if man builds his relationship with God on the right foundations. Islam provides those foundations.

---

1. For a detailed study of the Muslim contribution to science and technology, see S. Hossein Nasr, *Science and Civilization in Islam*, Cambridge, 1966; and *Islamic Science — An Illustrated Study*, London, 1976; *The Legacy of Islam*, new edition (1975) edited by J. Schacht and C. E. Bosworth; S. Cobb, *Islamic Contribution to Civilization*, Washington, 1965.

Muslim Population of the World

(A) MUSLIM COUNTRIES IN ASIA

Name	Muslim Population	Muslim Percentage
1. AFGHANISTAN	17,721,000	99%
2. BAHRAIN	220,000	99%
3. BANGLADESH	63,750,000	85%
4. BRUNEI	114,000	76%
5. INDONESIA	125,127,000	95%
6. IRAN	31,571,000	98%
7. IRAQ	9,657,000	95%
8. JORDAN	2,429,000	95%
9. KUWAIT	917,000	100%
10. LEBANON	1,722,000	57%
11. MALAYSIA	5,925,000	52%
12. MALDIVE ISLANDS	125,000	100%
13. OMAN	750,000	100%
14. PAKISTAN	62,945,000	97%
15. QATAR	170,000	100%
16. SAUDI ARABIA	8,175,000	100%
17. SYRIA	5,994,000	87%
18. TURKEY	37,620,000	99%
19. UNITED ARAB EMIRATES	320,000	100%
20. YEMEN ARAB REPUBLIC	1,440,000	95%
21. YEMEN P.D.R.	6,000,000	99%

(B) MUSLIM STATES/AREAS IN ASIA UNDER NON-MUSLIM CONTROL

State/Area	Muslim Population	Percentage	Political Status
1. AZERBAIJAN	7,023,000	78%	*Under* USSR
2. INDIA	65,000,000	12%	*Under* India
3. KASHMIR	5,164,000	78%	*Under* military occupation of India
4. KAZAKHSTAN	8,738,000	68%	*Under* USSR
5. KIRGHIZIA	2,699,000	92%	*Under* USSR
6. PALESTINE	2,612,000	87%	*Under* the occupation of Israel

(B) MUSLIM STATES/AREAS IN ASIA UNDER NON-MUSLIM CONTROL (continued)

State/Area	Muslim Population	Percentage	Political Status
7. SINKIANG	7,535,000	82%	*Under* China
8. TAJIKISTAN	2,842,000	98%	*Under* USSR
9. TURKMENIA	1,943,000	90%	*Under* USSR
10 UZBEKISTAN	36,669,000	88%	*Under* USSR

(C) MUSLIM CONTRIES IN AFRICA

Name	Muslim Population	Muslim Percentage
1. ALGERIA	15,386,000	98%
2. CAMEROUN	3,365,000	55%
3. CENTRAL AFRICAN REP.	902,000	55%
4. CHAD	3,400,000	85%
5. DAHOMEY	1,746,000	60%
6. EGYPT	33,387,000	93%
7. GABON	234,000	45%
8. GAMBIA	327,000	85%
9. GUINEA	4,047,000	95%
10. GUINEA BISSAU	567,000	70%
11. IVORY COAST	2,484,000	55%
12. LIBYA	2,178,000	100%
13. MALI	4,853,000	90%
14. MAURITANIA	1,227,000	100%
15. MOROCCO	16,826,000	99%
16. NIGER	3,963,000	91%
17. NIGERIA	59,820,000	75%
18. SENEGAL	3,819,000	95%
19. SIERRA LEONE	1,800,000	65%
20. SOMALIA	4,000,000	100%
21. SUDAN	14,375,000	85%
22. TANZANIA	9,347,000	65%
23. TOGO	1,166,000	55%
24. TUNISIA	5,245,000	95%
25. UPPER VOLTA	3,879,000	56%

(D) SIGNIFICANT MUSLIM POPULATION AND MUSLIM AREAS UNDER NON-MUSLIM RULE IN AFRICA

	Country/Area	Population	Muslim Percentage
1.	ANGOLA	1,450,000	25%
2.	BURUNDI	720,000	20%
3.	COMORS ISLANDS	286,000	95%
4.	EQUATORIAL GUINEA	75,000	25%
5.	ERITREA	2,250,000	75%
6.	ETHIOPIA	17,289,000	65%
7.	GHANA	2,808,000	30%
8.	KENYA	3,682,000	29.5%
9.	LIBERIA	498,000	30%
10.	MALAGASY REPUBLIC	1,350,000	20%
11.	MALAWI	1,677,000	35%
12.	MOZAMBIQUE	2,205,000	29%
13.	UGANDA	3,881,000	35.9%

(E) MUSLIM POPULATION IN EUROPE

Country	Muslim Population 1975	Muslims as % of Total Population
a. NON-COMMUNIST		
1. ANDORRA	3,000	15%
2. AUSTRIA	50,000	Less than 1%
3. BELGIUM	150,000	1.5%
4. CYPRUS	180,000	33%
5. DENMARK	20,000	Less than 1%
6. FINLAND	4,000	Less than 1%
7. FRANCE	1,972,830	3.8%
8. GERMANY (WEST)	1,500,000	2.4%
9. GIBRALTAR	3,000	10%
10. GREECE	270,000	3%
11. IRELAND	500	Less than 1%
12. ITALY	517,000	1%
13. LUXEMBURG	1,000	Less than 1%
14. MALTA	36,670	11.4%

Country	Muslim Population 1975	Muslims as % of Total Population
15. NETHERLANDS	200,000	1.5%
16. NORWAY	6,000	Less than 1%
17. PORTUGAL	5,000	Less than 1%
18. RHODES	16,000	Less than 1%
19. SPAIN	25,000	Less than 1%
20. SWEDEN	10,000	Less than 1%
21. SWITZERLAND	60,000	Less than 1%
22. UNITED KINGDOM	1,000,000	1.7%

b. COMMUNIST

Country	Muslim Population 1975	Muslims as % of Total Population
23. ALBANIA	1,763,000	75%
24. BULGARIA	1,207,000	14%
25. CZECHOSLOVAKIA	150,000	1%
26. HUNGARY	105,000	1%
27. POLAND	661,400	2%
28. RUMANIA	188,000	Less than 1%
29. YUGOSLAVIA	3,770,000	18%

c. UNDER RUSSIAN CONTROL

Country	Muslim Population 1975	Muslims as % of Total Population
30. BASHKIR	240,000	60%
31. CHUVASH	900,000	60%
32. CRIMEA	2,676,500	53%
33. MARI	412,500	55%
34. MORDOVIA	650,000	52%
35. TARTAR	2,075,000	65%
36. UDMURAT	1,100,000	55%
37. UKRAINE	5,657,000	12%

(F) MUSLIMS IN AMERICA AND OTHER PLACES

Country	Muslim Population	Muslims as % of Total Population
1. ARGENTINA	486,000	2%
2. AUSTRALIA	132,000	1%
3. BRAZIL	210,000	0.2%
4. CANADA	100,000	0.5%
5. CHILE	50,000	0.05%
6. FIJI ISLANDS	60,000	11%
7. GUYANA	114,000	15%
8. MEXICO	10,000	0.02%
9. NEW ZEALAND	20,000	0.6%
10. PANAMA	50,000	3.5%
11. TRINIDAD AND TOBAGO	127,000	12%
12. UNITED STATES OF AMERICA	3,169,000	1.5%

TOTAL MUSLIM POPULATION 907,197,000

Note: The information about the Muslim population has been derived from a number of Muslim and non-Muslim sources. The main sources on which we have relied heavily are, however, the *World Muslim Gazetteer,* Umma Publication, 1975, Karachi and *Muslims in Europe,* compiled by Khurshid Ahmad for the Islamic Council of Europe, 1976.

SELECTED BIBLIOGRAPHY

(a) Qur'ān:

Pickthall, Muhammad Marmaduke, *The Meaning of the Glorious Qur'ān* (Arabic text with English translation), Taj Company Ltd., Karachi.

'Alī, 'Abdullāh Yūsuf, *The Holy Qur'ān* (Arabic text with English translation and some explanatory notes), Beirut, 1973.

Mawdūdi, Abul A'la, *The Meaning of the Qur'ān,* (Arabic text with English translation of his Urdu Qur'ānic exegesis called *Tafhīm al-Qur'ān)* Vols 1-5 (incomplete) Lahore, 1967-76.

47

(b) Ḥadīth:

Bukhārī, Muḥammad bin Ismāʿīl al-Bukhārī (d. 256/869) *Al-Jāmiʿ al-Ṣaḥīḥ*, English translation by Dr. M. Muhsin Khan, 9 vols., 2nd edition, 1973, Madina.

Muslim, Muslim bin al-Ḥajjāj (d. 261/874) *Kitāb al-Ṣaḥīḥ*. English translation by A. H. Siddiqi, Lahore, 1973.

Abū Dāwūd, Abū Dāwūd Sulaymān al-Ashʿath (d. 275/888) *Kitāb al-Sunan*, various editions.

Ibn Māja, Muḥammad bin Yazīd b. Māja (d. 273/886) *Kitāb al-Sunan*, several editions.

Nasāʾī Aḥmad bin Shuʿayb al-Nasāʾī (d. 303/913) *Kitāb al-Sunan*, several editions.

Tirmidhī, Muḥammad binʿĪsā al-Tirmidhī (d. 275/888) *Al-Jāmiʿ al-Ṣaḥīḥ*, several editions.

Mishkāt, Ibn al-Farrāʾ al-Baghawī (d. 516/1122) revised by Walī al-Dīn ʿAbdallāh al-Khaṭīb al-Tibrīzī in 737/1239 and titled *Mishkāt al-Maṣābīḥ*. English translation in 4 vols. by James Robson, Lahore, 1972.

Fiqh:

al-Jazīrī, ʿAbd al-Raḥmān, *Kitāb al-Fiqh ʿalā Madhāhib al- ʿArbaʿa*, Cairo. Urdu translation by Manzur Ahsan ʿAbbāsī, Punjab, Lahore.

Kāmil, ʿAbdul ʿAzīz, *Everyday Fiqh*, Vol. I, Islamic Publications, Lahore, 1975 (based on Mawlānā Yūsuf Iṣlāḥī's Urdu text *"Āsān Fiqh"*).

Islam: General:

Mawdudī, Abul Aʿlā, *Towards Understanding Islam*, Nairobi, Islamic Foundation, 1976.

Ahmad, Khurshid (ed.), *Islam: Its Meaning and Message*, Islamic Council of Europe, London, 1976.

Hamidullah, Muhammad, *Introduction to Islam*, Paris, 1959.

Qutb, Muhammad, *Islam: The Misunderstood Religion*, Kuwait, 1967.